DO IT *YOURSELF!*

Today, DIY is a hugely popular pastime, and there is a ready supply of well-made products on the market that are easy to use. This means that you, whether a homeowner or apartment dweller, can get a sense of achievement by dealing with problems yourself, and also save money by not having to call in professionals every time a window creaks or a door begins to rattle.

This book provides the basic information you need to look after your home in a handy-to-use format.

HarperEssentials

BIBLE GUIDE
CARD GAMES
DIY (DO-IT-YOURSELF) TIPS
FAMILY AND PARTY GAMES
FIRST AID
STRESS SURVIVAL GUIDE
THE ULTIMATE SURVIVAL GUIDE
UNDERSTANDING DREAMS
WINE GUIDE
YOGA
ZODIAC SIGNS

HARPERESSENTIALS

DIY
(DO-IT-YOURSELF)
TIPS

HarperTorch
An Imprint of HarperCollins*Publishers*

Please Note: Always take care when embarking on any DIY project. Read the instructions before you commence and take appropriate safety precautions.

This book was originally published by HarperCollins UK in 2004.

Based on material from *Collins Complete DIY Manual by Inklink, Tommy Walsh DIY Survival*, and *Collins Ultimate Home Solutions*.

HARPERTORCH
An Imprint of HarperCollins*Publishers*
10 East 53rd Street
New York, New York 10022-5299

First HarperTorch paperback printing: April 2005

CONTENTS

INTRODUCTION

Today, DIY is a hugely popular pastime, and there is a ready supply of well-made products and materials on the market that are easy to use. This means that you, as a homeowner, can get a sense of achievement by dealing with problems yourself, and also save money by not having to call in professionals every time a door begins to rattle.

This book provides the basic information you need to look after your home in a handy-to-use format. It begins by covering the basic tools you will need, what hardware is necessary for attaching or constructing items and how to locate the main services in your house. The next chapters concentrate on the areas in which you can carry out maintenance and repairs yourself. The chapter on decorating techniques emphasizes the need for good preparation, then provides a guide to choosing the right products and using the correct techniques. The book ends with vital information on how to make your home as secure and cost-efficient as possible.

TOOLS

INTRODUCTION

Before getting started you need to ensure you have the right tools for the job you are about to tackle.

ESSENTIAL TOOLKIT

There are some basic essential tools that every toolkit should contain. Some of these are multi-purpose and can be used for a variety of DIY jobs.

It is important to look after your tools, so that they last for as long as possible. Store them neatly and ensure that they are kept in good condition. Blunt blades are dangerous to use so dispose of them carefully. You can sharpen handtools, but power tools are best serviced by professionals.

Level This straightedge is used to check whether a structure is level, either horizontally or vertically. The glass tubes in the level contain liquid with a floating air bubble. When the bubble is positioned between the two lines marked on the tube, this indicates that the structure is exactly level.

Tape measure Essential for marking out measurements, a tape measure that can be locked open is the best option. Try to buy one that is about 16 feet long.

Square This is used for marking right angles on wood before cutting as well as for checking the accuracy of jointed corners and planed timber. It is worth buying the largest one that you can afford.

Awl An awl is used to make a starter hole in timber before inserting a screw.

TIP: It is always best to spend as much as you can afford on tools as the top-quality ones are really worth the investment. They will do the job well and, as long as you keep them clean and store them neatly, should last a long time.

Claw hammer This general-purpose hammer is the one you will use the most. The claw is used for levering out nails. Buy one with a steel rather than wooden shaft.

Pin hammer
This lightweight hammer is used for tapping in panel pins and tacks—hence its name.

Adjustable wrench
An adjustable wrench can be used to fit around any sized nut, to tighten or loosen it as necessary.

TIP: Power tools are extremely expensive so, unless you plan to use them a lot, it makes sense to rent them when necessary.

Screwdrivers It is important to have a number of different screwdrivers as you must match the size and shape of the driver to the screw. Some screws have slotted heads while others have cross-heads and there are screwdrivers specifically designed to be used with each.

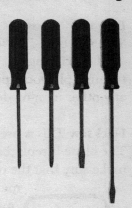

Clamps These are generally used to hold pieces of glued wood together while they set. They can also be used to assemble structures temporarily to check that everything fits properly or to hold small workpieces together while you are working on them.

Cordless drill This makes light work of drilling and does away with the need for a long extension cord. It is best to choose one with a variable-speed facility for inserting woodscrews and a hammer action for drilling into masonry.

Bow saw
This saw is
used for cutting
through plywood, pressboard and
any other man-made boards.

Hacksaw This is used for cutting through metal.
The blade is replaceable and you should always
make sure that the one you use is harder than the
metal you are cutting through. A
mini hacksaw, shown here, is
used for cutting
tubing or small metal
piping.

Tenon saw This
general-purpose,
small-toothed saw is
used for woodwork
and joinery.

Miter saw A miter saw has slots at
various angles,
which makes
cutting an
angled joint
very straight-
forward.

Protective gloves Safety should always come first and gloves can protect your hands from cuts. They should also always be worn if you are using chemicals.

Ear protectors These should be worn when you are breaking up concrete, sanding a floor or doing any other excessively noisy job.

Dust mask Whenever the work you are doing creates a lot of dust, you should wear a mask to protect your mouth and nose.

Safety glasses Again, if there is a lot of dust around, flying particles such as paint, or you are using chemicals, wear glasses in order to protect your eyes.

HARDWARE

Whenever attaching or constructing anything, it is vital to choose the right type of hardware to ensure that the item doesn't come loose at a later date.

NAILS AND SCREWS

Nails are cheap and simple, but quite crude, so for anything that requires strength or is going to be permanent you should use a screw. If you are going to be fixing a screw into a wall you will also need to use an anchor plug, or "molly."

Nails There are many different types of nails for both general and specific purposes. To ensure the best hold possible you need to choose the right kind and size.

Plugs These go into drilled holes and then screws are driven into them. This means that the plugs effectively act as anchors for the screws.

Screws These can have cross-heads or slotted heads and come in a range of sizes. They are usually made of mild steel, but there are also solid brass and stainless-steel screws that do not rust.

DRILL BITS AND TAPE

There are many drill bits that attach to electric drills. You will also discover that tape is vital.

Wood bits These allow you to drill into wood.

Masonry bits These bits enable you to drill through masonry.

Masking tape This is useful for masking off areas, such as those you want to paint, to ensure the rest of the surface is protected.

HSS bits These are used for drilling through metal.

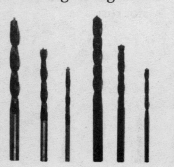

Duct tape This tape is waterproof so is very handy for all sorts of jobs, including plumbing.

GLUES AND ADHESIVES

Adhesives today are far better than the glues that were used in the past. With the correct adhesive it is possible to bond together just about anything.

Wood glue This is specifically for gluing pieces of wood together.

Sealant While some sealants also act as adhesives, generally sealant is not an alternative to glue. Instead it is used as a seal between two surfaces, and can be flexible, waterproof and even colored.

Multi-purpose adhesive While there are specific adhesives for gluing metal, glass, masonry, rubber, etc., there are also multi-purpose adhesives on the market that are much more versatile.

ATTACHING PIECES OF WOOD

+ To nail two pieces of wood together securely, you will need a nail that is long enough to pass at least halfway through the piece of wood that you are nailing into. If the joint is going to be bearing any load, you should strengthen it by spreading wood adhesive onto the surfaces in contact before nailing. Hammer the nail into the first piece then position the second carefully before driving the nail right in, until its head sits just above the wood surface. Then drive the head just below the surface using a nail punch. To finish off, put wood filler in the hole and then sand the surface when it is set. To complete the attachment, repeat the process with as many nails as necessary.

+ An alternative to nails, instant-grabbing adhesive is especially useful in areas that are hard to reach and where nails would be unsightly. Simply squeeze small blobs of the adhesive onto the surfaces you wish to attach and stick them together.

+ To screw two pieces of wood together, select a countersunk screw that is, again, long enough to pass through the second piece of wood that you are driving the screw into. Position the pieces of wood together and then drill a pilot hole of about $1/13$ inch in diameter right through the top piece and halfway through the bottom piece. Pull the pieces apart and drill a clearance hole of ⅛ inch in diameter through the top piece. Put the countersink bit into your drill and use it to drill the necessary countersink shape in the mouth of the clearance hole. Position the pieces of wood back together, insert the screw into the hole and drive it in using a screwdriver until its head is flush with the surface of the wood. Repeat the process for all other screws being used.

SECURING HARDWARE TO WALLS

• When securing shelf battens, brackets or curtain fixtures to solid walls, use screws and anchor plugs. The screws should be long enough to penetrate the wall by at least 2 inches. Always use the thickest screws possible.

• With timber-framed walls there are two approaches. For putting up single shelves that will be holding only light items, you can use screws and special plugs that splay out once they've passed through the plasterboard in order to hold the screws in place. For any other shelves, kitchen cupboards, etc., you need to drive the screws into the vertical timber frames within the wall, which are called studs. You can use a stud finder to locate these, or knock on the wall—it will sound hollow until you reach a stud and then the knocking will become duller.

IDENTIFYING SERVICES

It is vital to know where all the main services (water, gas and electricity) are in your home so you know where to switch things off before doing any electrical or plumbing work and also in case of an emergency.

WATER

Locating your shut-off valves

In an emergency you may need to cut off the water supply to your home, or you might need to work on a particular part of the plumbing system and therefore want to isolate it. The following valves will enable you to do this:

Water company valve This is normally found at the property boundary and can be used to shut off the supply to the house. In urban areas, it is often located under the street and should be accessed only by water company personnel.

Mains valve This is usually located under the kitchen

sink but may be elsewhere. It turns off the supply for the house but leaves the tank full of water.

Other stop valves There are valves on radiators, cold-water pipes to garden taps, washing machines and dishwashers, which will isolate that particular appliance or tap for repairs.

Switching off and draining the system

You may need to drain and refill your central heating if you wish to move a radiator, or if there is a problem that needs to be fixed. Most systems have at least one drain plug located at the lowest point in the system, which allows you to empty the water, but there may be others by the boiler and in other low pipework.

To drain the system:
+ Turn off the water heater and/or boiler.
+ Turn off the mains valve and, if possible, the water company one too.
+ Turn on all taps to drain the water from the pipes.
+ Attach a hose to each drain plug in turn, ensuring the hose reaches outside or to a bath. Use a wrench to unscrew the drain plug so all the water flows out.
+ Unscrew the air bleed valves on the radiators and hot-water tank.

To refill the system:

✦ Close all the drain plugs and air bleed valves before turning on the mains valve.

✦ As the system fills, turn on the taps to allow water and air to escape. Then bleed each radiator.

✦ With the system refilled, turn the boiler on and check that there are no leaks from any of the valves. Tighten them where necessary.

GAS

Most homes are supplied with mains gas, which runs through underground pipes in the streets

straight to the gas meter within each property. The meter is usually in the basement, although recently gas companies have begun to fit meters in boxes outside, fixed onto exterior walls. The mains gas on/off valve is situated on the supply pipe

just before the meter. It is on when the handle is in line with the pipe, and can be switched off by turning the handle 90 degrees.

IF YOU SMELL GAS

If you think you have a gas leak you should never try to deal with it yourself. *Do not switch on any lights or electrical appliances* and *do not strike a match*. Turn off the gas valve and ensure everyone has left the house. Then call your gas company's emergency number.

Gas boilers

Most larger homes employ the indirect water system, which uses a gas boiler and a copper cylinder where the water is heated up (top right). Many of these have pilot lights that are on constantly, in order to ignite the burners whenever heat is needed. The gas combination boiler, on the other hand, is often used in a smaller property (right). This only heats the water when it is required so does not have a storage system. You should always ensure you read the manufacturer's instructions on how to start your boiler up and control its timer.

TIP: Boilers must be serviced regularly to ensure that they are running correctly. There is normally a written record next to the boiler indicating when services were done and when the next one is due. Any gas work, including the servicing, should only be undertaken by a registered contractor.

PLUMBING

Although some people are nervous about tackling their house's plumbing system there are many jobs that can be simply and easily carried out. And in an emergency, you will probably need to repair the problem temporarily while you wait for the plumber.

PLUMBING TOOLS

You may find the following tools necessary if you are going to undertake plumbing work.

Hydraulic pump Similar to a plunger, this can be used to unblock a waste pipe. It is hand-operated and a downward push will create a jet of water that may push the obstruction clear. An upward movement, on the other hand, may create enough suction to pull the obstruction back out.

Drain rods These can be rented if your plumbing system's main drains and inspection chambers need to be cleaned out.

Auger An auger is designed to clear toilets and is rotated using a handle.

Monkey wrench This wrench has adjustable toothed jaws that can be tightened to grip pipework.

Vise grips This is useful for gripping pipework or damaged nuts and it is also often used as a small clamp. The adjustable screw at the end of the handle tightens the grip.

Radiator key This is used to release trapped air within a radiator. When attached to the bleed valve on the radiator, the key is simply turned counterclockwise to release the air.

ELECTRICITY

There are many simple electrical jobs that can be undertaken by homeowners, as long as you exercise caution, follow instructions and use the right tools.

ELECTRICAL TOOLS

Long-nose pliers These pliers have extra long noses so they can be used in tight, hard-to-reach spaces. They can be used for gripping items firmly.

Combination pliers This multi-purpose tool does the job of both pliers and wire cutters.

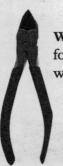

Wire cutters These are useful for cutting through cables and wiring.

Wire strippers These are used to remove insulation from cable and flex.

Insulated screwdriver This type of screwdriver is used for tightening electrical terminals and so has a long cylindrical shaft with a flat tip.

Electrical tape This plastic tape can be used around wiring because it is insulated.

TIP: Although there are electrical jobs you can carry out yourself, if you are in any doubt about what you are doing you should stop and contact a professional electrician.

FLOORS AND STAIRS

Wooden floors and stairs do get damaged by general wear and tear so every so often you will probably need to carry out some simple repairs to specific areas.

REPLACING OR REPAIRING DAMAGED FLOORBOARDS

There is a trend these days to utilize existing floorboards as floorcoverings rather than carpet. This will undoubtedly mean that some of the boards need replacing, simply because of their age. They may be affected by termites, woodworm, dry or wet rot (all of which will require treatment), may have dried out and shrunk slightly to produce gaps or may have been split when raised by workmen to gain access to piping and wiring. If a board has more than a couple of holes in it you should replace it.

You will find it easier to lift the damaged boards if you first remove the baseboard fitted around the area of the floorboards. However it is possible to free boards without removing the baseboard, by lifting the ends until they are almost 90 degrees against the baseboard, then pulling the board free from between the baseboard and joist. Try to choose one of the shortest lengths to start with. Use crowbars or a bolster chisel inserted at opposite sides of the center of the board to lever it upward (1). If you need extra leverage, place a wooden block under each crowbar. This will also protect the floorboard from damage (2). Repeat the process along the length of the wood. Once the first board is out, you will have easier access to remove the other damaged boards. If the boards are only partially damaged you can then simply cut out the affected parts. Once a board is raised up, place two wooden battens underneath it to support it. Then you can mark around the damaged section using a square (3—page 24).

1. Insert a crowbar to start levering out the first board. Be very careful as you do this.

2. Place a wooden block under the crowbar for extra leverage and to protect the board.

3. Use a square to mark around the damaged area before removing it with a tenon saw.

4. Once you have tapped the new piece of board into position, nail it down firmly.

Cut out this section using a tenon saw before laying the rest of it back down. Mark and cut out a matching piece from a new board. Cut this about 1/13 inch too long, to ensure that it will fit tightly without gaps when it is in position. Use a wooden block and hammer to tap it into place. Finish off by nailing the new board and remaining part of the old one into place with brad nails (4) and smooth with a sander or sandpaper.

TIP: If you are going to be using the floorboards as your only floorcovering, when replacing boards try to find second-hand ones that match the others, or make sure that you stain the new boards to match once they are in position.

CURING GAPS IN FLOORBOARDS

If there are some gaps between your floorboards it is best to close these up to ensure that the floor is draftproof. If there are lots of gaps that are widely spaced you will probably need to re-lay the whole floor (*see* below).

If, however, there are just a few gaps then you can fill them with thin pieces of wood. For each one, measure across the gap then trim the edge off a spare board to create the sliver, planing it to the correct size. Apply wood glue to the gap then tap the sliver into position with a mallet or small hammer. Plane or sand it to make it flush with the surrounding boards.

Re-laying floorboards

If you have a lot of damaged boards (due to fire damage or timber decay) you will need to replace them with new ones. Alternatively you may just have large gaps between the existing boards, which means ripping them up and re-laying them. The method of laying both new and old boards is the same.

> **TIP:** If you are re-laying an entire floor rather than just a smaller section, you will probably need to clamp the boards in place as you go along. Special floorboard clamps can be rented for this job.

Once the floor has been completely taken up you will need to lay down a few loose boards over the joists to use as a working platform. Then remove any old nails from the joists using crowbars and a claw hammer (1). Lay out four to six boards at a time, laying them ⅜ inch short of the walls to leave an expansion gap and room for the baseboard. Ensure you use a mix of short and long lengths and stagger where the joints will be as you don't want joints occurring next to each other.

Drill fine pilot holes into the boards to prevent any splitting and also to indicate where the nails should go (2). Then use floor brad nails in pairs about

1. Remove old nails from the joists using a claw hammer.

2. Use a drill to create pilot holes for where the nails will go.

3. Use brad nails to secure the boards.

1 inch from the edges to hold the boards in place (3). You can use a nail punch to drive the nails beneath the surface.

TIP: When you are laying new floorboards, it is a good idea to lightly mark on them with pencil the position of pipes so that you avoid puncturing the pipes when you nail the boards into place.

SHEET FLOORING

If you need to replace a whole floor of boards, but will be covering them over with carpet or laminate, it is worth considering sheet flooring as a cheaper alternative to boards. This usually comes in sheets of 8 x 4 feet.

Plywood Exterior-grade plywood is suitable for flooring. When laying plywood directly onto joists, ensure it is $5/8$–$3/4$ inch thick.

Chipboard Flooring-grade chipboard is more compressed than other types. It comes in $3/4$-inch and $7/8$-inch thicknesses. Use the first on joists spaced no more than 16 inches apart and the second on joists spaced at 2 foot intervals.

MDF This is available in a variety of thicknesses. It is more expensive than chipboard but cheaper than plywood.

REPAIRING AND REPLACING DAMAGED BASEBOARD

A baseboard is both practical and decorative as it provides a "kick board" between the floors and walls and conceals necessary expansion gaps. Over time, therefore, baseboards do receive a lot of damage and parts will eventually need to be repaired or replaced.

Repairing damaged baseboard

Sometimes you can simply cut out the damaged piece of baseboard and replace that small part without having to pull the whole thing apart. Knock the blade of a small bolster chisel behind the baseboard to create a gap big enough to slot a crowbar into. Place a couple of pieces of wood down behind the baseboard to keep it away from the wall (1). You could also put a thin piece of wood behind the crowbar to protect the wall.

Now position a miter box against the baseboard and use the 45-degree slot to cut the baseboard with a tenon saw, using short strokes to protect against damage (2).

Repeat the whole process at the other side of the damaged piece, cutting the 45-degree angle in the opposite direction, then remove it. Take the pieces of wood out from behind the baseboard and then use a drill to countersink and screw the remaining baseboard back into its original position. Next measure out a replacement piece of baseboard, put it into position and start tapping pins in to hold it in place. Add a bead of wood glue along the top then knock the pins in completely (3).

1. Insert pieces of wood to keep the baseboard away from the wall.

To finish off, use a pin punch to drive the pins below the surface of the baseboard and wipe away any excess wood glue. Use filler on the pin holes, screwheads and joints; give this time to dry and then sand everything down. The final thing you need to do is paint the new piece of baseboard the same color as the rest of the baseboard so that it matches.

2. Use a miter box to cut the damaged piece out.

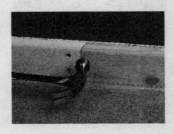

3. Fix the new piece of baseboard into position.

Replacing baseboard

If you have to remove all the baseboard in a room in order to replace it, start with the same method of levering the first piece free (*see* page 28). Once that is out the rest should be much simpler to dislodge.

You will need to cut internal and external miter joints, so investing in a miter saw is a good idea. (Be aware that it does take time to master how to use such a saw so it is worth practicing on scrap wood before undertaking a job.) Measure each wall length in turn and mark them onto the new baseboard, also marking a 45-degree angle for the miters where necessary. Cut these out (1) then begin to position the pieces.

1. Use a miter saw to cut the internal and external angles in the new baseboard.

2. You can use masonry nails to fix the baseboard directly into masonry or brickwork.

> **TIP:** When you are pinning through a miter, it is a good idea to make a pilot hole first by putting a pin into your drill and using it like a drill bit. This is because a miter is quite delicate and could easily split.

The new baseboard may be fixed directly into masonry or brickwork using masonry nails (2). However you may find it easier to put battens onto the walls and then simply fix the baseboard onto these. While the internal miters can simply be fixed with masonry nails, the external miters must be pinned together in order to ensure that the joint fits together perfectly (3). For extra strengthening, it is also a good idea to add a couple of pins through the edge of each miter joint (4).

3. Glue then pin the external miters to ensure that the joints fit together well.

4. Drive pins directly through the miters to provide extra strengthening.

CURING SQUEAKY STAIRS

In the majority of our homes, stairs are made of wood, which shrinks over time because it dries out. When the various components within a staircase shrink, the joints are loosened with creaking and squeaking being the unfortunate result.

Before starting any repairs it is vital to know what the various components of a staircase are and where to find them. The diagram below indicates the main elements.

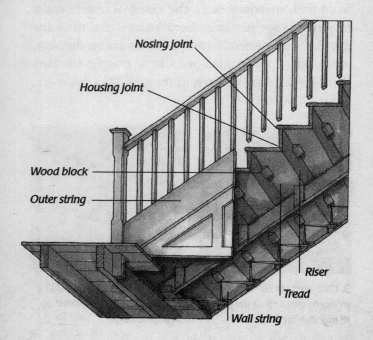

Nosing joint

Housing joint

Wood block

Outer string

Riser

Tread

Wall string

It is possible to cure the squeaks from both above or below the stairs, although it is usually best to work from below if at all possible because a better repair can usually be carried out from behind.

To find out exactly where the problem lies, ask someone to walk slowly up the steps while you are positioned at the underside of the stairs so that you can note where the loose steps are and take a closer look for the source of the squeak.

Sorting loose blocks

If one of the triangular blocks that fit between the treads and risers has worked loose, remove it and clean off any old adhesive. Next, pry the shoulder of the joint open a little to apply wood adhesive (1). Then apply new adhesive to the block and position it in the joint, moving it back and forth

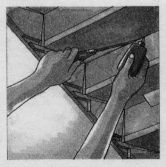

1. Pry the joint open to apply wood adhesive to it.

2. Apply adhesive to the wood block and then reposition it.

slightly until it is fixed securely (2—page 33). If you feel this hasn't worked satisfactorily you can also use panel pins to hold the block in place while the adhesive sets.

> **TIP:** If any of the blocks are missing or badly damaged, cut new ones out of 2 x 2-inch softwood.

MENDING A LOOSE HOUSING JOINT

If the tread or riser has become loose in its string housing, the glued wedge may also be loose. Use a chisel to pry this out (1) then clean it up. Apply wood adhesive to the joint before driving the wedge back in with a hammer (2). If the wedge is too damaged, make a new one out of hardwood.

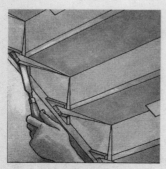

1. Pry the loose wedge out from the string housing.

2. Apply adhesive to the joint and drive the wedge back in.

Curing a loose nosing joint

Sometimes a squeak will occur because a nosing joint has come slightly loose. To cure this, you can use countersunk screws (*see* pages 12–13). Drill clearance holes, squeeze some wood adhesive into them and then insert and tighten the screws.

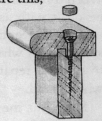

If these screws will not be concealed by a carpet, you should counterbore the holes so that the screwheads can sit beneath the surface of the tread. Then plug the holes with matching wood.

With the screws in place, fit wood into the holes.

Curing a loose riser joint

A loose joint at the back of a tread is more difficult to repair from above. You can try thinned-down wood adhesive in the joint but you won't be able to use screws to pull the joint together. You could reinforce the joint by using a section of triangular molding and gluing it between the tread and riser. You can only do this if the remaining width of the tread still meets the minimum requirement. As it won't look very neat, you should consider this only if the stairs are to be covered with carpet.

RENEWING NOSING ON WORN STEPS

Worn treads and nosings are dangerous and should be dealt with as soon as possible. As the wear is usually concentrated on the center of the step, since that is where people tread, you may be able to make a repair without having to take out the whole tread.

Mark out the area of the nosing that you need to cut with pencil cutting lines—one should be parallel with the edge of the nosing, just outside the damaged area, and the other two at right angles to it. Using a portable circular saw, adjust the blade depth to the thickness of the tread. Pin a batten parallel to the long cutting line to use as a guide for the saw's baseplate.

With the saw nose down, gradually lower it into the wood to make the cut along the length (1). Then use a tenon saw to cut the ends at 45 degrees to the tread face (2). Cut away the waste with a chisel, working against the grain and taking care not to damage the remaining tread and riser tongue (3).

Plane a groove in the underside of the new section of nosing to receive the tongue of the riser, and cut its ends to 45 degrees. Check that it fits correctly into the opening, then apply wood adhesive to all the meeting surfaces of the new nosing and riser. Clamp the nosing in position using a batten screwed into the tread at either end. You should place a piece of pressboard under the batten to increase the pressure and stop this from sticking with a piece of polythene (4).

Drill and insert glued dowels of ¼-inch diameter into the edge of the nosing to reinforce the joint. When the adhesive has set remove the batten then plane and sand the nosing so that it is flush.

1. Use the batten and cutting lines to guide the saw.

2. With the length cut, use a tenon saw to cut the ends at 45 degrees.

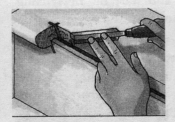

3. Use a chisel to remove any remaining waste from the area.

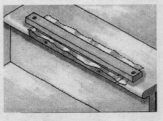

4. Check that it fits, then clamp the new nosing into position.

WINDOWS AND DOORS

The weather can play havoc with windows and doors over time but fortunately any repairs can be easily carried out by homeowners. Doors and door furniture are also items that are often replaced for aesthetic reasons when changing the decor in a whole room.

CURING A RATTLING WINDOW

Many windows today are casement windows, which are especially vulnerable to the weather. Often the sash (the part of a window that opens) distorts over time and begins to rattle. You can move the catch plate of the lever fastener to pull the sash tighter into the frame. Use a screwdriver to undo the catch plate (1). Hold it in its new position and use an awl to mark and start off new fixing holes (2). Secure it into place with the screws.

1. Undo the catch plate with a screwdriver.

2. Use an awl to mark the new fixing holes.

CURING A STICKING WINDOW

When windows stick most people simply force them open time and time again without fixing the problem. However, this could damage the sash construction so try the following methods instead.

Using candle wax

Try smearing candle wax on both the edge of the window and the frame to allow them to glide together more easily without sticking.

Run candle wax down the edge of the window.

Planing the edge

If using candle wax didn't help it may be that there is a build-up of paint on the window edge. Remove the paint and plane the edge so that it fits neatly against the frame. Once the window is operating well, paint the edge with primer, undercoat and top coat quickly to prevent damage to the raw wood (*see* page 81). Dry the paint between coats and then rub the surface with wax.

Plane the edge until it fits neatly against the frame.

REPLACING A WINDOWPANE

A cracked or smashed windowpane is a safety hazard and security risk. The damaged pane will no longer be weatherproof either, so it must be replaced as quickly as possible.

1. Lever the beads out from the frame.

Replacing a pane in a beaded window

Some window frames have screwed-on beading that has been embedded into compound. This beading holds the panels in place.

Before you start this job you must make sure that you put on thick gloves and goggles for protection. Then, starting from

2. Place the pane into the frame.

3. Fix the beads back in using pins.

the top, use a hammer and chisel to gently lever out the beads from the frame (1). Remove the glass, bit by bit, as you work around the frame. Clean off any remaining compound from the frame then seal the exposed wood with wood primer (*see* page 88). Measure the inside of the frame and then ask the glazier to cut your new glass ⅛ inch smaller on each dimension to provide a tolerance for fitting.

Run compound around the inside of the frame then place the lower edge of the pane onto the bottom of the frame (2). Press the pane into position. Fix the beads back in place with pins, starting with the top one, then the bottom and finally the side beads (3). Use a nail punch to drive the pins in and then fill and sand the holes before repainting if necessary.

Replacing a pane in a puttied window

Again, make sure you wear thick gloves and goggles before removing the broken windowpane. It is a good idea to place strips of tape over the pane as this will hold the broken pieces in place (1—page 43).

Old dry putty will usually come away easily, but for any stronger bits you will need to cut and chip them out using a glazier's hacking knife and hammer (2—page 43). It is always safest to work from the top down. Pull out any sprigs (wedge-shaped nails) that you come across. Clean off any putty remnants from the frame and then seal the wood with a wood primer.

Have the new piece of glass cut ⅛ inch smaller than the dimensions as before to provide tolerance when fitting. Take a palm-sized ball of putty and work it up to an even consistency. (For jobs like this it is generally easiest to use universal putty. It will need a bit of kneading before it is applied.) Press a line of it into the insides of the frame to a depth of about ⅛ inch (3).

Lower the edge of the glass into the bottom of the frame. Press the pane into the putty and secure it with sprigs, tapping them flat against the glass with a chisel edge. Trim the resulting surplus putty with a putty knife. Apply a thick, even layer of putty to the outside of the frame (4) and use the knife to create a smooth finish of 45 degrees, mitering the corners. Let the putty set completely before painting it, removing any paint marks from the glass.

TIP: You should always take a piece of the original glass with you when getting a professional glazier to cut the new panes so that they can match the thickness. The glazier will also be able to advise you on how much putty you will need for your job if you want to use traditional linseed-oil putty instead of the universal type.

1. Put strips of tape over the pane to hold the shards of broken glass as you remove them.

2. Old putty should come away easily but chip out any bits that seem to be stuck.

3. Press a ⅑ -inch deep line of putty around the edges of the frame.

4. With the new glass in place, apply a final layer of putty to the outside of the frame.

REPLACING BROKEN SASH CORDS

With sash windows, it is most often the cords that the sliding sashes are suspended from that break or wear with time.

When this happens the window will become difficult to open and will judder when raised. It is best to replace all the cords, even if only one is broken. Before starting this type of job you will need to know a bit more about the workings of a sash window, which are detailed here.

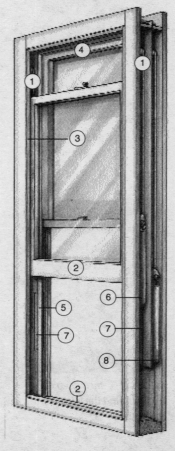

1. Pulleys
2. Bottom sash
3. Staff bead
4. Top sash
5. Parting bead
6. Bottom sash weight
7. Pocket
8. Top sash weight

Removing the sashes

Lower both sashes and cut through the cords with a knife to release the weights. Lower the weights as far as possible before allowing them to drop. Use a chisel or paint scraper to pry off the staff beads from inside the frame, starting in the middle of each bead.

Lean the inner sash toward you and mark the ends of the cord grooves. Reposition the sash and transfer the marks onto the pulley stiles. Pull the sash out of the frame then pry away the narrow parting beads. Mark the ends of the grooves in the top sash then take it out.

Unscrew the weight pockets (bits of wood at the bottom of each side of the frame) to reveal the weights. Lift these out. Remove the old sash cords from the weights.

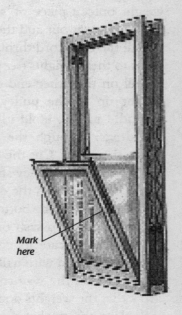

Mark
here

Mark the cord grooves.

Refitting the sashes

The sash cords and weights are put in place before the sashes are refitted. Measure each sash for the new sash cords and cut these to length, allowing roughly ¾ inch for trimming. Start with the top sash and where the old, cut-off cord is still in place you can tie this to the new length to draw it through the pulley. Where it is broken, tie a small weight onto a piece of string, pass this over the pulley, lower it out and then the string can be used to pull the new cord through (1). Tie the new sash cords to their weights (*see* page 47).

Pull on the other end of the cord to move the weight up to the pulley, then let it drop back around 4 inches. Hold it here temporarily with a nail driven through the cord into the stile just below the pulley. Cut the cord level with the mark you made on the pulley stile (2). Follow this procedure for the cord on the other side of the top sash and then both on the bottom sash.

Replace the top sash on the sill first, leaning it toward you. Locate its cords then nail them into place with round wire nails. Nail just the bottom 6 inches, not all the way round (3). Lift the sash to check that the weights do not touch the bottom.

Replace the pocket pieces and pin the parting beads back. Fit the bottom sash the same way then replace all the staff beads.

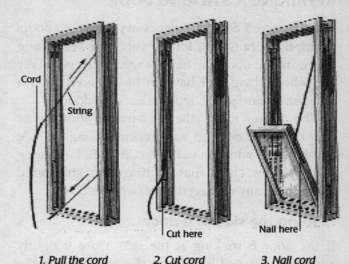

1. Pull the cord through.

2. Cut cord at mark.

3. Nail cord to sash.

Tying a sash knot

To make the correct figure-eight knot, make a loop in the cord at about 3 inches from the end. Take the end round the back of the cord to form the figure eight and then pass it through the first loop.

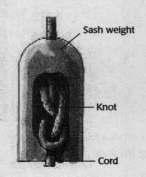

REPAIRING A STICKING DOOR

Make sure you deal with necessary repairs to doors promptly, because the longer you leave something the more the door will be damaged, and eventually the whole thing will have to be replaced. It is a straightforward job to repair a sticking door.

The change in weather as summer draws near may cause the door to start sticking along the side and bottom, which is easily rectified. Before doing this, however, check that the hinges are still sound and replace any damaged ones (*see* page 55).

Planing the side of a door

If the door is sticking at the side, close it tightly and mark a pencil line down the edge against the jamb (1). (The jamb is made up of the two verti-

1. Mark a line down the edge of the door.

2. Use a hand plane on the edge.

cals on either side of the doorframe and the horizontal along the top.) This will show where the door needs easing back.

Use a hand plane to plane off the high points until the edge is the same distance from the pencil line all the way down the side of the door (2).

TIP: Sometimes it is a build-up of paint on the door edge that causes the problem. To solve this you can use a heat gun to take off the excess before planing the surface smooth.

Planing the door base

If it is sticking along the bottom, close the door and use a piece of cardboard and a pencil to mark a line along the bottom. This will indicate where any tight points are. Then take the door off its hinges and plane off these points before refitting the door and checking that it no longer sticks.

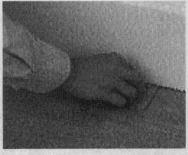

Mark a line along the bottom of the door.

Adjusting hinges

You may need to adjust the hinges slightly to square the door onto the frame. Sometimes, however, the hinges have been cut in too deep, which results in the door binding on the frame. The adjustment here entails packing out the hinges. To do this, remove the door and hinges (1), wedging the door with small wedges so it stays in the open position.

Cut small shims from thin cardboard that will fit behind the hinges (2), then place the shims into position (3) before screwing the hinges back into place. This will adjust your door toward the jamb. You may find that you need more than one piece of cardboard so you should screw the hinges back one screw at a time so that you can easily close the door to check the fit. Add or remove bits of card-

1. Remove the door and its hinges.

2. Cut small shims from thin cardboard.

board until the door fits perfectly. Then fix the rest of the screws back to hold the hinges tightly.

STRENGTHENING A HINGE

When a door has been taken off and refixed a few times over the years, the screws in the fixing holes usually loosen and then the hinges themselves come loose. To strengthen the hinges, take the screws and hinges out of the holes, then pare down some softwood to form dowels. Place wood glue onto the ends and tap these dowels into the holes. When the adhesive has set, cut off any excess dowel and reposition the hinges. It is best to screw these down into the dowels to create a firm fixing.

TIP: After years of wear, hinges and their pins/screws can become slack. Rather than buying new hinges you can swap the old ones round, which will reverse the wear on the pins.

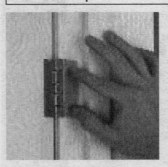

3. Place the shims behind the hinges.

REPAIRING A RATTLING DOOR

If a door is rattling it means it isn't meeting the stop or jamb properly. You will need to remove and reposition each part of the jamb to create a neat fit.

Use a hammer and chisel to gently tap the joint between the jamb and frame to ease it off. Remove all the nails. Now close the door. Reposition the jamb, starting with the first vertical so that it allows the door to close snugly. Check this then nail it into place securely. Reposition the other vertical and top jamb in the same way.

Reposition the jamb and use nails to fix it into place.

REPLACING A DOOR

When you need to replace a door with a new one, you must measure the height and width of the door opening as well as the depth of the rebate in the frame. It is best if you can find a door of the correct size, but you can trim the door down if you can't locate one. You will need to check that the door fits into the frame neatly anyway before fixing the hinges into place and this could result in a few necessary trims.

Cutting a door to size

New doors often have "horn" extensions on their stiles (the upright sides) to prevent the corners from being damaged in transit. You will need to cut these off first (1). Transfer the measurements you took from the door opening onto the door itself, making allowances for the necessary clearances (*see* box on page 54).

1. Saw off the horn extensions from the stiles.

2. Plane the door down to the right size.

3. Use wedges to try the door in the frame.

To reduce the width of the door, clamp it on its edge in a portable workbench (to keep it steady) and then plane it down to the marked line. If you need to remove a lot of wood, take it off both stiles. (This is especially important for panel doors, as this will preserve the symmetry.)

To reduce the height of the door by more than ¼ inch use a saw to take off the bulk of the waste and then finish off the job with a plane. Otherwise you can just trim the door to size using a sharpened plane (2—page 53). To avoid chipping the corners out by mistake, work from each corner toward the center. Finally, support the door on small wedges (3—page 53) to see if it fits in the frame. Make any further adjustments as necessary.

MEASUREMENTS

The figures provided here should be used as a guide when trimming the door and positioning the hinges.

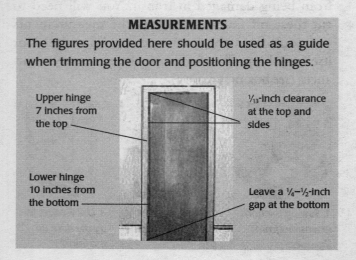

Upper hinge 7 inches from the top

$\frac{1}{13}$-inch clearance at the top and sides

Lower hinge 10 inches from the bottom

Leave a ¼–½-inch gap at the bottom

Fitting hinges

The hinges should be positioned equally into the stile and doorframe. Wedge the door in the opening at the correct floor clearance level then mark the appropriate positions for the hinges (*see* box on page 54) on both the door and frame. Stand the door on its edge with the hinge stile at the top. Open one hinge and align one flap on the marks made on the door edge before drawing around it with a pencil (1). Hold a hinge against a combination square and adjust the ruler on the square to the depth of the hinge. Hold the square perpendicular to the door edge and mark the depth of the recess.

1. Mark around the flap using a pencil.

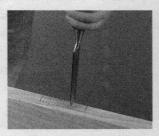
2. Use a chisel to cut out the recess.

3. Mark the size of the flap onto the doorframe.

Use a chisel to make a series of cuts across the grain and then pare out the waste up to the scored lines (2—page 55). Repeat the process for the position of the second hinge. Use the flaps again as guides to drill pilot holes for the screws. Fix both hinges into their recesses. Wedge the door back into its open position in the frame then align the free hinge flaps with the marks made on the doorframe. Ensure that the knuckles of the hinges are parallel with the frame, then mark out the recesses (3—page 55). Cut these out using the same method as for the recesses on the door edge. Hang the door, using just one screw per hinge, to check whether you need to make any adjustments. Doors and frames are often not completely square, so you may need to make the recesses deeper, or pack out the hinges with cardboard (*see* pages 50–51). When you are happy the door is opening and closing properly, drive the rest of the screws in.

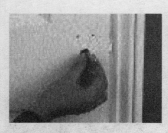

1. With the handle plates removed the spindle is visible.

2. With the handle plate on, mark the positions of the fixing holes.

REPLACING A DOOR HANDLE

Try and choose a new handle that fits over the screw holes left behind by the old one (you may even be able to utilize the old holes). Remove the old handle by loosening the screws on each handle plate. This will leave just the square spindle still in place (1). Work on one side of the door at a time, positioning the new handle over the spindle to see if the spindle needs cutting down (so the new handle plate will sit flush with the door). Cut the spindle with a hacksaw, if necessary, then put the new handle plate on and check that it is level. Mark where the fixing holes should be with an awl (2) then drill small pilot holes for the screws (3). Screw the handle to the door and check it with a level (4), making any necessary adjustments. Then fix the other handle to the other side in the same way.

3. Drill pilot holes for the screws that will hold the handle.

4. With the handle in position, check it with a level.

FITTING DOOR FURNITURE

Door furniture includes the door knob, knocker and mail slot. You should always try to purchase good-quality hardware as you'll find cheap ones don't last for long.

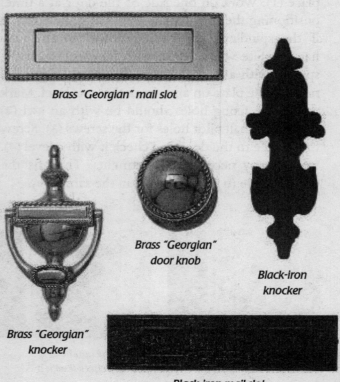

Brass "Georgian" mail slot

Brass "Georgian" door knob

Black-iron knocker

Brass "Georgian" knocker

Black-iron mail slot

A door knob

External door knobs are usually placed on the central line of a panelled door, often above a mail slot.

Drill a counterbored hole from the inside. This type of hole allows the head of a screw to lie below a surface—here it will take the head of the screw that will be used to fix the knob in place. It is also the clearance hole for the threaded shank that will need to pass through the door. The backplate of the knob will have a locating peg on its reverse to stop the knob from turning when the screw is tightened. Drill a shallow recess for this peg, then fit the knob and tighten up the screw. You can plug the counterbored hole on the inside to create a neat finish.

Counterbore the hole for the fixing screw.

A door knocker

This isn't seen as essential nowadays, but is often added as a decorative item for a traditional look. To fit one, hold the knocker in place and then press it hard against the door in order to leave positional marks. Then drill a counterbored clearance hole for the fixing screw in the same way as you would for a door knob (*see* page 59). Plug the hole on the inside after the backplate has been fitted.

FITTING FINGER PLATES

Finger plates are designed to protect the paintwork on interior doors. They are very straight-forward to fit—simply screw them to each side of the door so that they sit just above the handles.

A mail slot

These come in all sorts of styles, sizes and materials. They are usually fitted horizontally, although the method described here can be used to fit a vertical one as well.

Decide where you want the mail slot to be. On a panelled door it is often fitted horizontally on the middle cross rail. Draw around the outline of the mail slot with a pencil. Measure the size of the hinged flap and closing spring and mark the outline of the required rectangular slot within the first outline, ensuring it is just slightly larger than the hinged flap and spring (1). Drill a ½-inch access hole in each corner of the outline and use them to saw along the outline with a padsaw or power jig-saw. Once you have cut out the slot, trim its corners with a chisel.

Mark out positions for the fixing holes then drill counterbored holes to attach the mail slot (2) using the same method you used for attaching the door knob and knocker (*see* pages 59–60). You may find you have to shorten the screws if your door is thin. Plug or fill the holes from the inside or fit an internal flap cover.

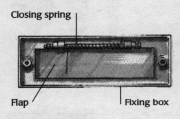

Closing spring

Flap

Fixing box

1. Use the dimensions of the flap and spring to work out the required rectangular slot.

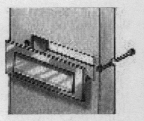

2. Create counterbored holes that the slot's screws can then be fitted into.

TIP: A mail slot can sometimes create a draft in the hallway as wind whistles through the opening. You can screw a draftproofing plastic flap to the edge of the plate on the inside of the door. This often also has nylon bristles to help keep out the cold air.

DECORATING TECHNIQUES

A room can be completely transformed by employing the simple techniques described in these pages.

DECORATING TOOLS

Here are details of some of the
basic decorating tools available.

Paintbrushes These come in a
range of sizes and the brushes
can be made from animal hair
or synthetics.

Paint roller and tray When
painting a large area, a roller
and tray are ideal. Load the
roller from the deep end of
the tray, then run it up
and down to distribute
the paint evenly.

> **TIP:** When using water-based paints, you can clean
> paintbrushes with warm, soapy water. Brushes that
> have had oil-based paints on them must be cleaned
> with turpentine.

Sponge This is used for wiping down surfaces to ensure that they are completely clean before applying new decoration to them.

Steam stripper If you are stripping a lot of wallpaper it makes sense to buy one of these, but you can also rent them. The steam that is generated helps to lift the paper off the wall.

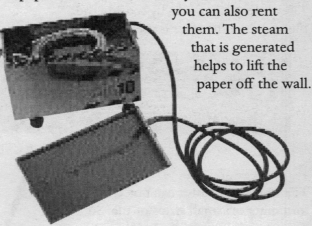

Orbital scorer A scorer can be run across a wallpapered wall to punch small perforations through the paper. This then allows the steam or water to penetrate the wallpaper much faster.

Heavy-duty scraper There are various scrapers for removing paint and wallpaper. This heavy-duty one lifts wallpaper with ease.

Tile cutter This works by scoring the tile and then the lever is used to snap it.

Tile nippers A cutter can't be used for taking off small strips of tile. So once the tile is scored using the cutter the waste can be removed bit by bit using nippers.

Grout spreader/float A rubber spreader allows you to spread tile adhesive evenly between laid tiles.

PREPARING WALLS FOR DECORATION

It is vital to undertake preparations thoroughly, so that you have a solid base on which to decorate. Walls, particularly older ones, will never be perfect so you should rectify any problems before applying your chosen decoration. If you don't, old dents and marks will still show through the decoration. Also, certain problems won't go away just because a new layer of paint is hiding them. So deal with small problems now to avoid their getting any worse.

Filling cracks, dents and holes

If large cracks and holes in plaster aren't dealt with they will eventually reappear. Start by raking out any loose material from the crack or hole with a scraper (1).

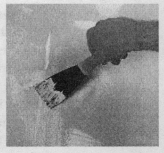

1. Rake out all the loose material with a scraper.

2. Press cellulose filler into the crack.

Try not to insert your scraper right down into the crack or hole as you will just cause more plaster to fall off. (You want to get rid of only the really loose plaster as you do this.) On largish cracks you will need to cut across from the sides to the center to create a key for the filler.

Use a paintbrush to dampen down the crack, then press cellulose filler into the crack using a filling knife. Drag the blade across the crack so that the filler is forced right down into it (2—page 65) and then use the knife to smooth the surface off, leaving it slightly raised. Leave the filler to set and then use fine-grade sandpaper to rub the surface smooth and flush.

Filling small holes in plasterboard

There are two ways that you can mend holes in plasterboard. You could use plasterer's glass-fiber patching tape on holes up to 3 inches across. Simply stick the self-adhesive strips in a star shape over the hole, then apply cellulose filler and feather the edges to create a smooth finish (1).

Alternatively, you can use an offcut of plasterboard that is just larger than the hole but narrow enough to slot through it. Make a hole in the middle of the offcut so that you can then thread a piece of string through it and tie a nail to one end of this (2). Butter the ends of the offcut with filler before feeding it into the hole. Then simply pull on the string to force the offcut hard up against the plasterboard (3)—the filler will help keep it in place. Press extra filler over the top until it is almost flush with the surface. Give the filler time to set and then cut off the string before applying a

1. Fill the patch with patching tape and apply filler.

2. Fix string to the offcut and tie a nail onto the string.

3. Pull on the string to force the offcut into position.

final thin layer of filler, which will create a flush, smooth finish.

Repairing edges

Cracks can occur in the edges between walls or a wall and ceiling and these can be filled with a thin line of filler (*see* opposite). However the external corners of walls see more damage because they are prone to being knocked. To fill any chips right on the edge, pin a temporary wooden batten to create a straight edge then fill the hole with filler using a filling knife (1). Once the filler is dry take the batten off and fill the pinholes. When this filler has dried, sand down the surface (2).

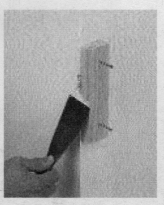

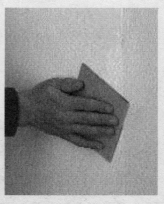

1. Use a batten to create a straight edge, then fill the hole.

2. When the filler is completely dry lightly sand the surface.

Filling gaps with caulk

Decorator's caulk is a flexible filler that is applied using a mastic gun. It is great for filling gaps between walls, walls and baseboard or around doors and windows.

Start by cutting off the tip of the nozzle, then apply the caulk in a steady line across the gap (1). Release the trigger on the gun when you've reached the end. Smooth off the caulk with a damp sponge, which you will need to rinse out regularly (2).

1. Run a line of caulk along the gap.

2. Use a damp cloth to smooth the caulk.

WASHING DOWN WALLS

When you have made all the necessary repairs to the walls, sanded them all smooth and swept up the resulting dust, you should wash the walls down with a damp sponge. This will remove any lingering residue or debris.

STRIPPING WALLPAPER

Before you start, empty out the room and roll up carpets and underlay to avoid damaging them. Score the walls with a scraper or orbital scorer (1). Then soak the paper with warm water and a sponge. The more you soak it, the easier it will be to remove. This takes time but you can concentrate on stripping one wall while soaking the next one so it is ready when you've finished the first. To speed things up, use a steam stripper. Make sure you follow the manufacturer's instructions very carefully (2). Don't hold the steamer

1. Score the paper with an orbital scorer or scraper.

2. You can use a steam stripper but follow the instructions carefully.

over one area for too long or you may cause the plaster underneath to loosen. Once one area has been steamed, move the steamer on to the next bit and use a scraper to take off the loosened paper (3).

Some papers will allow you to strip off the face and leave the backing intact, which can be left on. If this isn't sound, remove it by soaking it with warm, slightly soapy water applied with a paddle brush (4). Do two thorough soakings before scraping the paper off. To finish, clear up all the waste and then wash the walls down with warm, slightly soapy water again.

3. It is easy to remove the steamed paper with a scraper.

4. Apply soapy water to the backing paper with a paddle brush.

PRIMING SURFACES

Once all the wall surfaces are prepared, they need to be primed and sealed so that they are able to accept the finish that you have chosen.

The chart on pages 74–75 covers all the primers and sealers that you are likely to use around your home. Refer to this to find out which one is appropriate for the job that you are about to undertake. You can then read the further details about it that are provided below.

Types of primer and sealer

There are many types of primers and sealers that can be used on a variety of different surfaces.

Stabilizing primer This is used to bind together powdery or flaky surfaces. It is usually a white or clear liquid.

General-purpose primer This seals porous surfaces and covers patchy walls and ceilings. Certain general-purpose primers are suitable for use on wood, metal and plaster.

Metal primers These prevent corrosion and certain special rust-inhibitive primers will also treat rust and then prevent its recurrence. Metal primers also provide a key for paint.

Water repellent This liquid is used to seal masonry against water. It dries colorless.

Alkali-resistant primer This primer is used to stop the alkali that is found in some surfaces from attacking oil-based paints.

Aluminum spirit-based sealer The fine scales of aluminum form a barrier to stop materials that are likely to "bleed." This sealer is effective over bituminous paints, creosote and metallic paints.

Stain sealer This creates a permanent seal against problem stains such as nicotine, water, soot, crayon, lipstick and ballpoint pen.

Panel-system primer This primer provides a better adhesion for masonry paints that are applied to building boards. Used alongside polyester scrim, it can reinforce repaired cracks in exterior render.

The table provided below indicates the various surfaces that each of the primers and sealers can be effectively used on.

PRIMERS AND SEALERS

SUITABLE FOR	STABILIZING PRIMER	GENERAL-PURPOSE PRIMER	ZINC-PHOSPHATE PRIMER	FAST-DRYING METAL PRIMER	RUST-INHIBITIVE PRIMER
Brick	●	●			
Stone	●	●			
Cement rendering	●	●			
Concrete	●	●			
Plaster	●	●			
Plasterboard	●	●			
Distemper	●				
Limewash	●				
Cement paint	●				
Bitumen-based paints					
Asbestos cement	●	●			
Ferrous metals (interior)			●		●
Ferrous metals (exterior)			●		●
Galvanized metal			●	●	
Aluminum			●	●	
Drying time (Hours)					
Touch dry	3	4–6	4	0.5	2
Recoatable	16	16	16	6	6

● Black dot indicates that the primer and surface are compatible.

PVA BONDING AGENT	WATER REPELLENT	ALKALI-RESISTANT PRIMER	ALUMINUM SPIRIT-BASED SEALER	STAIN SEALER	PANEL-SYSTEM PRIMER
●	●	●			
●	●	●			
●	●	●			●
●	●	●			
●		●		●	
		●		●	
●			●		
●		●			
3	1	4	0.25	2–3	–
16	16	16	1	6–8	24

TYPES OF PAINT

There is an enormous range of paints and finishes available for decorating today, and it can sometimes be confusing when you are faced with such a large choice. What follows is a basic introduction to paint and the different types that can be used for interior decoration.

All paints are made up of solid pigment suspended in a liquid binder, which allows it to be applied onto a wall easily. This binder then forms a solid film when dry. The term "finish" refers to any such liquid substance that, when dry, protects and often colors surfaces.

Common paints and additives

Oil-based paint This is made up of a mixture of oil and resin. Examples include primers, satin and gloss paints and metal paints.

Water-based paint Emulsions are the best-known water-based paint. They are made from a synthetic

---

FALSE ECONOMY

Cheap paints may seem like a real bargain but they have less pigment in them. This means that you will probably need to use several coats and buy extra cans.

resin that is dispersed in water. Most dry with a mid-sheen finish. Examples include matte and silk vinyl emulsion and acrylic satin paints.

Paint additives As well as binder and pigment, paints also include additives, which can make them dry quicker, drip less and last for longer.

Paints for interior decoration

Most interior walls are plastered and emulsion paint is normally the preferred choice. However there are other paints available to create a textured surface or to provide a particular degree of protection on a wall.

EMULSION PAINTS

These are practical paints for walls and ceilings, as they are relatively cheap and almost odorless. They are available with matte or satin (semi-gloss) finishes and some are non-drip too.

✦ **One-coat emulsion** This provides a good finish without your having to use the normal two coats of paint. Don't try to spread it too thinly though, or it won't be effective.

✦ **New-plaster emulsions** These are specifically designed for newly plastered walls, as they allow moisture vapor to escape.

+ Anti-mold emulsion This contains a fungicide that blocks out the staining caused by minor mold growth and deters regrowth. If you do have a problem with mold in a room, you shouldn't rely on this to solve it—deal with the cause of the damp.

GLOSS AND SATIN PAINTS

These are primarily intended for use on woodwork but gloss and satin paints are also available to

TYPE OF PAINT	USAGE	FINISH
OIL-BASED		
Primer	Wood/metal	Flat
Undercoat	Wood/metal/plaster	Semi-flat
Gloss	Wood/metal/plaster	High sheen
Eggshell	Woodwork	Satin
WATER-BASED		
Primer	Wood/metal	Flat
Undercoat	Wood/metal/plaster	Semi-flat
Satin finish	Wood/metal/plaster	Mid-sheen
Eggshell	Wood/metal/plaster	Mid-sheen
Vinyl matte emulsion	Plaster	Flat
Vinyl silk emulsion	Plaster	Mid-sheen
OTHERS		
Varnish	Woodwork	Various
Wood stain	Woodwork	Matte/silk
Knotting fluid	Woodwork	Matte/silk
PAINTS FOR METALS	There are a number of paints available, but by far	

use on any walls and ceilings that need a good degree of protection, because they are hard-wearing. As the name suggests, gloss has a very glossy finish while satin (or eggshell) is only slightly glossy.

TEXTURED PAINTS

These are good for disguising poor plasterwork, such as small cracks, and can also be used on masonry. There are matte or satin finishes available.

NOTES	CLEANING
Use this to seal bare wood	Turpentine
Apply this as a base for the top coat	Turpentine
Hard-wearing and durable	Turpentine
Hard-wearing and durable	Turpentine
Only use on interior woodwork	Soap and water
Apply before water-based top coat	Soap and water
Quick and relatively durable	Soap and water
Top coat for interior work	Soap and water
General-purpose coverage	Soap and water
General-purpose coverage	Soap and water
Available as water- or oil-based in a variety of finishes	Check label
Available as water- or oil-based in a variety of finishes	Check label
Used to seal knots in wood prior to finishing	Turpentine
the best paint to use is a hammerite-type paint designed for metal.	

COATS AND COVERAGE

Unless you are using a special one-coat paint you will need to build up layers of paint. How many you need, and the type of paint to use, depends on what surface you are trying to cover.

Painting walls These simply need one or two coats of the same paint to be covered sufficiently. Most emulsions, acrylic paints and solvent-based paints will leave patchy areas if only one coat is used.

PAINTS	Emulsion	One-coat emulsion	New-plaster emulsion	Solvent-based paint	Acrylic paint	Textured paint
NUMBER OF COATS (normal conditions)	2	1	2	1–2	1–2	1
DRYING TIME (in hours)						
Touch dry	1–2	3–4	1–2	2–4	1–2	24
Recoatable	4	–	4	16–18	4	–

Painting wood and metal These surfaces should be covered using a three-stage system that involves three different paints—primer, undercoat and top coat.

+ **Primer** seals the timber or metal. It is available as oil- or water-based and there are specific primers for wood and metals. However, if you have various surfaces to prime, a multi-purpose primer should do the job sufficiently well.

+ **Undercoat**—one or two coats will cover the color of the primer and also provide a key for the top coat.

+ **Top coat** is the final layer to go on and it provides a decorative finish and tough surface that will resist moisture, dirt and pollution.

The three-stage system uses three types of paint to cover metal or bare wood.

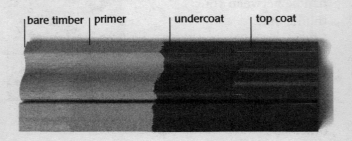

| bare timber | primer | undercoat | top coat |

PAINTING TECHNIQUES

When you are painting, work around the room in a logical manner and wait for each coat to dry before beginning the next one. There are some simple techniques you can follow to make the job easier.

Using a paintbrush

Always use a good-quality brush as cheap ones normally shed bristles. Don't overload the brush with paint—just dip the first third of the bristles into the paint and wipe off any excess against the edge of the paint can.

You can hold the brush in any comfortable position, but the "pen" grip is often the most versatile as it frees up your wrist to move in any direction it needs to. Hold the brush handle between your thumb and forefinger, with your fingers on the metal band and your thumb supporting the brush from the other side.

Hold the brush using the "pen" grip.

Using a roller

There are many different types of roller sleeves—long-haired ones are useful on textured surfaces, while lambswool sleeves are good for rolling on ceilings. There are also special rollers with extensions to help you reach ceilings and narrow rollers for use behind radiators. Pour the paint into a paint tray, then dip the roller into the paint reservoir at the bottom of the tray and roll it up and down the ribbed part to coat the roller evenly.

Apply the paint in a random crisscross pattern, ensuring you keep the whole roller in contact with the wall, to get an even coverage and then go over the whole area again rolling in one direction to finish.

Apply the paint using random strokes.

Using a paint pad

There are various sizes of paint pads available but one that is 8 inches long will apply paint evenly to walls and ceilings. Use a smaller one to "cut in" (*see* pages 84–85) at corners and ceilings. Paint pads are particularly useful for inexperienced decorators, as well as for painting large, flat areas. Load the pad from its paint tray, drawing it across the tray roller to ensure even coverage. Apply the paint by keeping the pad flat against the wall, sweeping it randomly but gently. To prevent streaking, finish off with light vertical strokes if you are using gloss paints.

Load the pad from its special tray.

TIP: Try to stop painting at dusk because if you work in poor light you are more likely to end up with a patchy finish.

Painting a room

As even the best professional will drip paint at some point, it is always best to start with the ceiling and work down. Make sure you have covered the floor and any furniture with dropclothes before you begin.

✦ **Painting the ceiling** Ceilings are best painted using a roller fitted with an extension lead if possible (or you can work on a sturdy work platform). However, as the roller won't go right to the edges you will need to start by painting these areas with a brush (1). This process is known as "cutting in." Then you can roller the main area of the ceiling (2).

✦ **Painting the walls** A roller is often the easiest way of getting paint onto walls as well, although you can use a brush or pad if you prefer. Paint in sections and always finish a whole wall before taking a break, otherwise there could be a noticeable change in tone somewhere on the wall. Emulsion paint can be painted in horizontal bands but gloss paint should be painted in vertical strips, because the joins between strips will be more noticeable unless you blend them in quickly.

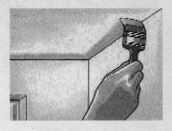

1. Cut in the edges with a brush.

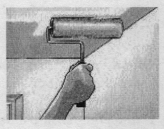

2. Roller the bulk of the ceiling area.

Cutting in is normally done before the main bulk of the painting but doing the wall cutting in at the end means you can get on with the rest of the painting while the ceiling is drying. This does require a steady hand though!

Cut in across the top of the wall.

Paints for metal

The most important part of painting metal is the priming, so that the paint will have a key to adhere to (*see* pages 72–73). After that, there are various finishes to choose from.

Solvent-based paints These are suitable for use on metal once an appropriate undercoat has been used.

Hammered-finish paints One-coat paints made of heat-hardened glass flakes, aluminum and resins.

Metallic paints Water-resistant, these paints provide a metallic finish due to the inclusion of aluminum, copper, gold or bronze powder in them.

Bitumen-based paints These can be used on exterior storage tanks and piping.

Security paints These stay slippery to stop intruders from using pipes to gain access to homes. Only for use on pipework more than 6½ feet off the ground.

Non-slip paints These provide secure footholding on metal staircase treads and fire escapes etc.

Painting radiators and pipes

You should turn off radiators and let them cool before painting them. They can then be painted with a brush. It is the back of a radiator that causes most problems. The best thing to do is remove the radiator completely, or swing it away from the wall. Alternatively, you can use a radiator roller or long-handled brush. These can also be used for painting in between the leaves of a double radiator.

Use a long-handled radiator brush to paint the hard-to-reach areas.

It is almost impossible to reach every part of a radiator, so concentrate on the bits that are seen. (Don't paint radiator valves or fittings!) Paint the pipework lengthways rather than across, otherwise runs will occur. You will need two or three coats, and let the paint dry before turning radiators back on.

PREPARING NEW WOOD

New wood usually comes ready primed, but it is worth ensuring that this is in a good condition. The safest option is to rub down the primer with fine-grade sandpaper, remove the dust and then apply a second coat of primer (*see* box below).

Unprimed timber should be sanded in the direction of the grain, dusted off and rubbed over with a rag moistened with turpentine. Then use the appropriate primer on the wood.

PRIMERS FOR WOOD

Wood primer This seals the pores in absorbent materials so that paint can't soak in when it is applied. Most hardwoods can be primed using this standard wood primer.

Acrylic wood primer This is quick-drying water-based primer. It can sometimes be used as an undercoat. It is used to prime softwood.

Aluminum wood primer This seals oily hardwoods and resinous softwoods.

Using grain filler

If you intend to use a clear varnish on open-grained timber, it is best to use a grain filler after sanding. Natural filler is fine for light timber but buy colored filler to match darker ones. Rub the filler across the grain using a coarse rag, leave it to set, then rub off the excess along the grain with a clean rag. Alternatively, you can apply successive coats of the clear finish and rub it down between coats until the grain is filled.

Use a rag to apply grain filler across the grain.

Sealing knots

Knots and any other resinous areas of the wood should be treated so that they don't bleed through and stain the subsequent painted surface.

Pick off any hard bits of resin then seal the knots by painting them with shellac knotting. You will need two coats. If you are going to paint the wood with a dark color, you could use an aluminum wood primer to seal knots and prime all in one go.

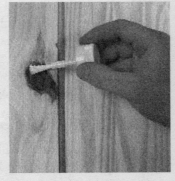

Seal any knots using shellac knotting.

PREPARING PAINTED WOOD

You may wish to paint areas of wood in your house that have been painted in the past. Sometimes you can use the existing paint as a base for the new paint, or you may have to strip the old paint off.

Sound paintwork

✦ If the paint is in a reasonable enough condition simply wash it, from the bottom upward, with warm water and gentle soap. Then rinse with clean water.

✦ Gloss paintwork should be rubbed down with fine-grade wet-and-dry sandpaper that has been dipped in water, in order to create a key.

✦ If there are any small patches of bare wood, prime them and then build up undercoat layers. Any open joints or holes will need to be filled.

✦ Reseal as necessary around window frames and doorframes using flexible filler.

Stripping weathered paintwork

Exposed paintwork will weather over time, becoming flaky, blistery or full of cracks. This paint will need to be removed. There are several methods of stripping.

+ **Heat stripping** You can use a hot-air gun to heat the paint so it can be removed with a scraper. Make sure you don't overheat the paint as you could burn the wood. Deposit the scrapings in an old metal container as they

Use a shavehook and hot-air gun to strip old paint.

will still be hot. An instrument called a shavehook will be needed to scrape moldings and more intricate areas.

+ **Chemical stripping** This takes more time but is best for fiddly projects and if you think the old paint contains lead (which is toxic). Cover the nearby floor, then apply a coat of stripper with a brush. Leave it for the indicated time then scrape a small patch to see if it has worked. Apply more stripper if not. Once it has worked, scrape the bulk of the paint away using a scraper and shavehook, then use steel wool dipped in the stripper to remove ingrained paint. Neutralize the stripper following the manufacturer's instructions.

+ **Industrial stripping** If you have a large but portable piece of wood, take it to a professional stripper to be immersed in a tank of caustic solution.

PAINTING WOODWORK

As wood is fibrous and different types have different rates of absorption you need to choose carefully the type of primer and paint to use. Wood can also be varnished, dyed or stained (*see* pages 94–95 for the relevant techniques).

Woodwork should be painted using a similar three-coat system to that used for metal (*see* page 81). Apply a coat of the relevant primer (*see* page 88) then, if you are using conventional solvent-based paint, you should apply one or two layers of undercoat depending on the coverage. As each coat hardens off, rub it down with fine wet-and-dry sandpaper to remove any blemishes, and then wipe over the surface with a cloth dampened with turpentine.

The final stage is the application of the top coat. You should use vertical brushstrokes to apply the paint, then spread it sideways to even out the coverage. Finish off with light strokes in the direction of the grain (this is known as "laying off"). You will probably need more

It is best to use vertical brushstrokes when applying the top coat.

than one coat and should blend the edges of the next application while the paint is still wet.

One-coat or acrylic paints should simply be laid on liberally with parallel strokes and laid off lightly. Make sure you blend wet edges quickly.

FINISHES FOR WOODWORK

	Solvent-based paint	Acrylic paint	Wood dye	Wood stain	Varnish
SUITABLE TO COVER					
Softwoods	●	●	●	●	●
Hardwoods	●	●	●	●	●
Oily hardwoods	●	●	●	●	●
Planed wood	●	●	●	●	●
DRYING TIME (Hours)					
Touch dry	4	1–2	0.5	0.5–4	2–4
Recoatable	16	4–6	6	4–16	14
NUMBER OF COATS					
Interior use	1–2	1–2	2–3	1–2	2–3
Exterior use	2–3	1–2	–	1–2	3–4

● *Black dot denotes compatibility. All surfaces must be clean, sound, dry and free from organic growth.*

STAINING AND VARNISHING

If you wish to leave wood unpainted you can use wood dye, stain or varnish to finish it off. Whichever you choose, prepare it in the same way, stripping any old finish then sanding the wood.

Applying wood dye

There are water- and oil-based dyes to choose from. If you are using a water-based dye you will need to carry out an extra preliminary stage—sand the wood then dampen the surface with a wet rag, let it dry and sand again. You can then use a brush, pad or lint-free rag to apply the dye. If you have a wide, flat surface use a 4-inch brush. Apply the dye liberally in the direction of the grain, quickly blending wet edges.

You can use a lint-free rag to apply wood dye.

Applying wood stain

The basic technique for applying wood stain is very straightforward. Shake the stain container and pour the liquid into a flat dish so you can load your brush properly. Apply the stain by working along the grain. You will need to work quickly and stain the edges at the same time as the top. The first layer of stain may appear patchy, but the second application will even out the color. If there are any powdery deposits left on the surface once a layer has dried, wipe them off with a coarse cloth before putting the next layer on. Leave the stain overnight then seal it with a clear finish.

Applying varnish

Varnish can protect wood from knocks and stains, and also gives a sheen that accentuates the grain pattern. It can be applied just like paint, by dipping the first third of the bristles of a paintbrush into the liquid then taking off the excess against the side of the container. Brush the varnish over the wood following the direction of the grain. If a brush is difficult to use, work it in with a lint-free rag instead. Leave it for the stipulated time and then apply a second coat. (If it has been left for more than 24 hours lightly key the surface of solvent-based glass varnish with fine-grade sandpaper and wipe down with a cloth.) You may need to apply a third coat.

Any minor imperfections, such as dust particles getting trapped in the varnished surface, can be rubbed down with sandpaper. To obtain a soft sheen you may want to add a layer of wax polish. Rub this in the direction of the grain using steel wool.

WALLPAPERING

Before you start it is important to clear a space and gather all the necessary equipment you will need for wallpapering, such as the paste, bucket, sponges, pasting brush and a table on which to apply the paste.

Mixing and applying paste

Many pastes are bought as powders or flakes, which then have to be mixed up with water. Do the mixing in a bucket, following the manufacturer's instructions. Tie a piece of string across the rim of the bucket to support the brush, which will help to keep the handle clean at all times.

If you are doing a lot of wallpapering, it is a good idea to invest in a fold-up pasting table, although any large flat surface will do. Lay several cut lengths of paper down on the table to keep it clean.

Align the wallpaper with the far edge of the table then apply paste with a pasting brush, working from the center outward. Once you have done a section, fold it over (but don't press it down) and slide the paper along till you reach an unpasted section. Once you have pasted the other end, fold it over to meet the first cut end. This second length is invariably longer than the first, and this is a handy way to tell which is the bottom end when you are working with patterned paper. Long drops of paper can be folded in an accordion fashion.

Some papers must be left to soak for a certain length of time while others should be hung immediately— check the manufacturer's instructions.

Fold up long drops into an accordion shape and leave to soak as needed.

TIP: Pre-cut enough pieces to cover a whole wall (bearing in mind that you may need extra to match up patterns), to enable speedy application.

The basic technique for wallpapering

You should start by deciding where the first piece of paper will be hung. This is often best placed next to a window, between two windows or over a prominent feature like a fireplace. Alternatively, you may want to deal with the largest wall first. As no wall is perfectly straight you will need to use a plumb line to mark a true vertical on the wall. Then place the first piece, allowing surplus paper for trimming top and bottom (1—page 98). (With this first piece absolutely vertical, all the others can follow it.) Brush from the center of the paper outward using a paper brush to remove any trapped air bubbles. Cut the top and bottom by tucking the paper right into the ceiling and baseboard with a straight edge, then trimming with a sharp craft knife or scissors (2). Repeat the process for the next piece, ensuring it butts up against the edge of the first piece as you brush out the air bubbles. Then use a damp sponge to remove any excess paste and continue around the room.

1. Leave surplus paper for trimming at either end of the paper.

2. Tuck the paper into the ceiling then trim it using a craft knife.

Papering around obstacles

There are simple techniques for creating clean lines of wallpaper when you are laying it around corners, radiators and switches.

✦ **Papering around corners** For an internal corner, cut a piece that covers the overlap piece from the first wall. For an external corner, trim the last length so it wraps around the corner, overlapping it by about 1 inch. Hang the next piece so that its edge is about ½ inch from the corner.

✦ **Papering around switches** Turn off the electricity at the mains fuse box first. Then hang the piece of wallpaper over the switch (or socket) and make diagonal cuts from the center of the fitting to each corner. Crease and trim the excess paper, leaving about ¼ inch all the way around. Loosen the faceplate and tuck the excess behind it before retightening the plate.

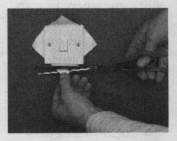

Trim off the waste, leaving a small amount to tuck behind the faceplate.

Wait for the paste to dry before turning the power back on.

✦ **Papering behind radiators** If you can't remove a radiator easily, which is the best option, you can cut the paper to shape, allowing about 4 inches to be smoothed behind the radiator. Then cut small pieces to fill the gap beneath the radiator.

FIXING WALL TILES

Preparation is the key to successful tiling. Spend time setting out the tile positions before you start laying them.

1. Make a gauge stick.

Fixing a batten

Measure the walls to work out where to start and how to avoid too many awkward cuts. The best way to do this is to make a gauge stick using a batten. Mark a row of tiles, with their spacers, on a length of softwood around 75 inches (1). Try to ensure that the cuts at the top, bottom and corners of the walls will be as equal and small as possible. Next, mark out the area on the first wall where all the whole tiles will be applied by fixing a

2. Fix horizontal and vertical battens on the wall as guides.

3. Press the tiles into the adhesive.

horizontal batten above the baseboard on the point you've chosen to start at. You should also fix a vertical batten near the corner (use a level to check the positions of both battens and screw them into place). These will be your guides (2).

Using a serrated spreader, apply adhesive over the wall, working about 3 foot square at a time. Press the tiles into the adhesive, using spacers as you go (3). With all the whole tiles in place, remove the battens ready for cutting and placing tiles around the edges.

Cutting tiles

Tiles can be cut easily with a tile cutter. To mark the first tile for cutting, hold it face down in position and mark it with a felt tip pen (allowing for spacers). Then place it in the cutter and score it first, before pressing on the lever to snap it. Position it on the wall and continue with the rest.

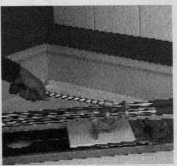

Use the lever on the cutter to snap the tile.

If you need to make any small cuts score the tile then use tile nippers to take away the waste bit by bit.

Grouting the tiles

With all the tiles in position, you should leave the adhesive to set for at least 24 hours. Then you can mix up the grouting material you have chosen, following the manufacturer's instructions. Next use a rubber grouting spreader, or float, to push the grout into all the joints (1). You should remove all the excess grout as you go with a damp sponge. (This will need to be rinsed out regularly.)

Sponging alone is enough to finish the joints, but compressing them will help waterproof the seal made by the grout. To do this, run along each joint with a jointer or end of a blunt stick (2). When the grout has dried, polish the tiles with a dry cloth.

1. Use a grouting spreader to spread grout into the joints.

2. Run along joints with a jointer to compress the grout further.

FITTING CURTAINS AND BLINDS

The window dressing is an important finishing touch to a room, so think carefully about what curtains or blinds you want to use.

Attaching a curtain rod

A wooden rod normally comes with two ring type brackets that the rod fits through. The rings fit into round wall fixings with holes in their centers. First, decide where you want your curtains to hang from and mark a line with a level. Mark the center of the window and position where your hardware will be.

You need screws that will fit through the plaster and masonry as well as the depth of the hole in the ring hardware. Drill your holes and insert wall-plugs then screw the round wall hardware to the wall. Now fit the wood support rings to the wall hardware, using screws. The rod needs to be threaded through the rings and the curtain rings placed onto the rod. Finally, fit the end stops onto the rod with their screws.

With the hardware in place, screw the wood support rings to them.

Hanging a curtain track

Measure the track and cut it to fit the window if necessary. Decide on the track's position using the method described on page 103. Tracks come with fixing brackets for the whole length, so screw these along the line. The track then simply snaps over the brackets (1). Now slide the gliders along the track and push and screw the stop gliders into place (2).

1. Snap the track over the brackets.

2. Screw the final gliders into place.

Fitting a window shade

A window shade can be hung within the window recess or across the front. Place the brackets in the top corners of the window frame if you are fitting it inside. Then cut the shade to fit. If fitting it outside, you will need to measure the shade and drill and plug the brackets into the wall at the appropriate places.

Now engage the square hole of the pull-cord end cap onto the control bracket, leaving the cords hanging down. Clip the other end into the opposite bracket. Identify which cord lowers the shade, fit a knob to it then pull the cord down level with the sill.

Remove the shade and unwind the fabric till it reaches the sill. Refit it and raise it to the open position with the other cord, then fit its knob. Check that the shade works well, adjusting the length of the cords if necessary.

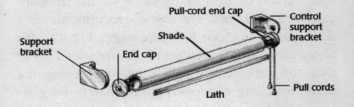

Fitting a venetian blind

To fit the blind into a window recess, measure the width at the top and bottom of the opening. If the dimensions differ use the smallest one. Allow for a clearance of about ⅜ inch at each end. Screw the brackets into place, setting the end brackets about 3 inches from the ends of the headrail. Mount the headrail in the brackets. Some may be clamped in while others need to be locked in place with a swivel catch. Finally, raise and lower the blind using the pull cord to check that it works properly.

HOME SECURITY

GUARDING-YOUR-HOME CHECKLIST

The risk of burglary is an ever-present part of life, but there are many things you can do to make your home more secure.

Front door Fit a mortise lock (*see* page 108) and a bolt top and bottom to the inside so that the door can't be forced open. For daytime security, also fit a door guard or chain lock (*see* pages 111–12). It's also a good idea to fit a peephole (*see* page 112) so that you can identify callers before opening the door. Installing outdoor lighting deters burglars too and aids identification.

Back and side doors Again, consider installing lighting, mortise locks and bolts. If the door opens outward then fit hinge bolts (*see* page 109).

Patio doors Any sliding doors would benefit from key-operated surface-mounted patio door locks.

Windows There is a range of locks available for both wooden and metal windows. The majority are surface-mounted. Fit key-operated locks to both downstairs and upstairs windows (*see* page 114).

Outbuildings Keep sheds, garages and other out-buildings locked, especially as they will probably contain tools and ladders that a burglar could use to break into your home! Standard door locks or padlocks can be used. If you have a side gate, lock it in the same way.

Downpipes Paint these with security paint to make it difficult for burglars to climb them (*see* page 87).

Burglar alarm Even a dummy alarm box can be enough to dissuade burglars. Alarms can be fitted by professionals but if you choose to fit one your-self make absolutely sure you have the practical skills to do so.

GOOD SECURITY HABITS

• Close and lock all windows and doors whenever you leave your house.
• Always use your alarm system, if you have one.
• If you are going out for the evening, draw curtains and leave lights on so it looks like you are in.
• If you are going on vacation ensure that it doesn't look like the house is empty. Ask a neighbor to pick up the mail and draw the curtains in the evening. You can also use automatic light timers to turn lights on at night.

CHOOSING THE RIGHT LOCK

Doors are vulnerable to forcing, which means you should consider using heavy-duty locks, especially on your front door. There are two main types for use on doors: rim and mortise locks.

Rim locks This type locks automatically when the door closes. One complete turn of the key prevents the lock from being operated from both outside and in. It is extremely hard to force open.

A cylinder rim lock

Mortise locks The body of a mortise lock fits into the edge of the door so it can't be tampered with easily. The heavy-duty bolt locks into the doorframe when the key is turned. You will need to know the width of your door edge when purchasing a mortise lock.

A mortise lock

FITTING HINGE AND RACK BOLTS

It is better to get a professional locksmith to fit the main locks to your front and back doors, but there are several extra measures you can fit yourself.

Fitting a hinge bolt

Hinge bolts are fitted from door to frame on the hinge side, hence their name. Start by drilling a hole on the inside door edge that is large enough to take the bolt (1). Mark a point on the frame directly in line with the hole and drill another one. Recess the locking plate into the frame so it fits over that hole. Most plates come with a paper template but if yours doesn't, hold the plate against the door to mark the area that needs to be recessed, then use a chisel to create the recess. Put the locking plate into position and screw it in (2).

1. Drill a hole that will fit the bolt.

2. Fix the locking plate to the frame.

Fitting a rack bolt

Rack bolts can be fitted into the edge of a door and are unobtrusive as well as secure. To fit one, drill a hole in the edge of the door big enough for the bolt body. Place a try square against the edge of the door, which provides a precise right angle to enable you to transfer the center of the hole to the inside face of the door. This will be the position of the keyhole so drill a hole here and then fit the bolt (1). Use the key to hold the bolt in place before marking the recess for the faceplate (2). Chisel this recess out. Screw the bolt and keyhole plate into position then close the door and operate the bolt to mark the doorframe. Drill a hole here to a depth that matches the bolt's length. Fit the locking plate over this hole before checking that the lock works properly.

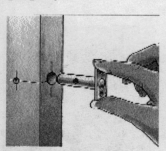

1. Drill a hole for the barrel and key then fit the bolt.

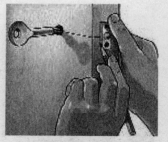

2. With the key holding the bolt, draw around the faceplate.

FITTING A DOOR GUARD AND PEEPHOLE

For added security fit a door guard or security chain, which allow you to open the door a small amount to check who is there. A peephole allows you to identify callers before you even open the door.

Fitting a door guard

A door guard is straightforward to fit and should be positioned a few centimeters above the door handle. The receiving bracket should be drilled and fixed to the doorframe using screws. The fixing plate may have to be recessed into the frame so that it finishes flush with the door. Position the bolt arm on the door and again use a drill and screws to fit it (1). Check that the bolt arm and receiving bracket are aligned correctly and make any necessary adjustments (2).

1. Attach both the receiving bracket and bolt arm with screws.

2. Check everything is aligned correctly and adjust as necessary.

SECURITY CHAINS

If you prefer to use a security chain instead of a bolt arm, it is very straightforward to fit. The fixing plates simply need to be screwed to the door and frame. The security chain should be positioned just below the lock.

Fitting a peephole viewer

When buying a peephole viewer, make sure you select one that has as wide an angle of vision as possible. Once it is fitted, you should be able to see someone standing to the side of the door or even crouching below the viewer. Also choose a viewer that is adjustable so it will fit any thickness of door.

To fit the viewer, first drill a hole of the recommended size (most viewers need a ½ inch hole) right through the center of the door at a comfortable eye level. Insert the barrel of the viewer through the hole from the outside then screw the eyepiece on from the inside.

An adjustable peephole viewer can be fitted to a door of any thickness.

WINDOW SECURITY

There are various security options for different windows. Casement windows are the simplest to fit locks to.

Fitting a lockable handle

A lockable handle can be attached to the opening edge of the window and the fixed frame. Mark the positions for the catch and handle, then make pilot holes for the screws using an awl. Screw the catch to the frame and the handle to the window.

Screw the catch and handle into position on the frame and window.

Fitting a swing lock

This is a neat, unobtrusive alternative to a handle. It is fitted in a similar way— the plate is screwed to the frame and the catch to the window. Check the alignment is correct before screwing the catch in tightly.

Screw the plate and catch into their final positions.

Security for sash windows

✦ You can use dual screws on sash windows. Each one consists of a bolt that passes through the window's meeting rails so that the sashes are immobilized. The

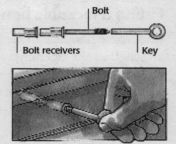

screw is then operated using a key. To fit one, keep the window shut and drill through the inner meeting rail into the outer one to the correct depth of the bolt receivers. Then slide the sashes

Use the key to turn the bolt until it is flush to the frame.

apart and tap the bolt receivers into their holes. Shut the window and use the key to insert the bolt until it is flush with the frame.

✦ If you open your sash windows a lot fit sash stops to the frames, which provide security but also allow them to be opened slightly. Drill a hole in the upper sash for

the bolt then screw the faceplate into place. Screw the protective plate to the top edge of the bottom sash.

A sash stop secures a window well.

SMOKE AND GAS ALARMS

These are essential to protect you and your family from smoke, fire and gas leaks.

Smoke alarms

There are two basic types of smoke alarms. Ionization alarms detect flames before the smoke gets too thick. These are the cheapest option. Optical alarms cost more and are better at detecting slow-burning, smoldering fires. The best place for a smoke alarm is on the ceiling, at least 1 foot away from any wall or light fitting. If you live in a single-floor home, fit it between the bedroom and living areas. To protect two or more floors, fit an alarm in the hallway and preferably one on each landing too.

Gas alarms

There are also devices that will detect gas leaks before the levels get dangerous. They should be positioned on a wall no more than 1 foot below the ceiling in the room where the main gas appliance is. Gas alarms should be wired directly to an unswitched fused connection unit that has a 3 amp fuse. If the alarm sounds, extinguish naked flames such as cigarettes and don't turn any lights on. Turn off the gas supply at its meter, then open all doors and windows before evacuating and calling your gas company from outside.

MONEY-SAVING TIPS

Conserving energy around the home is important for the environment. However, it is also one of the best ways of saving money on household bills. Most of us get used to leaving lights on all evening and using garden sprinklers in the summer. But there are simple ways to reduce energy waste without compromising on your comfort or pleasure.

REDUCING ELECTRICITY BILLS

Follow the checklist below to lower your electricity consumption, and save money.

Checklist

+ If you have electric heating, fit timer controls and thermostats (*see* pages 120–21) to keep control of how much electricity is used.
+ Switch off any lights when they are not needed.
+ Use low-energy light bulbs and low-voltage lighting, especially for lights that stay on for long periods. (Dimmer switches don't save money and you can't use the most energy-efficient bulbs with them either.) Compact fluorescent lamps cost more than ordinary bulbs but you

will recoup that money extremely quickly due to the amount of energy they save and their longer life.

+ If your big kitchen appliances (fridge, stove and dishwasher) are over ten years old, consider replacing them. Newer appliances are much more energy efficient and this will save you money in the long run.

+ Shut the fridge door promptly. Every minute it is open it takes three minutes to regain its temperature. Keep fridges and freezers as full as possible as this makes them most efficient.

+ Fridges should be set at 37 degrees F and freezers at -0 degrees F. Every degree lower than this adds about 5 per cent to the running costs.

+ Check the seals on the fridge and freezer doors. Empty the fridge and switch it off before you go on vacation.

+ Defrost your freezer regularly or if you are buying a new one choose a model that has an automatic defrost setting.

REDUCING WATER BILLS

There are many ways that you can cut down on your water consumption, as highlighted in the following checklist.

Checklist

+ Shower rather than having baths each day. A five-minute shower uses a third of the water that it takes to fill up a tub.

+ Always fix dripping taps promptly, as you could be wasting a bathful of water for each week that you leave them dripping.

+ Turn off the tap while you are brushing your teeth as otherwise you waste a surprising amount of water. (Running water can fill a small sink in five minutes.)

+ Run washing machines and dishwashers only when you have enough for full loads. A full load uses less water than two half-loads.

+ A third of most households' water is flushed down the toilet. (The equivalent of two baths a day is used for flushing.) Put a plastic jug filled with gravel in the toilet tank to reduce the amount of water stored.

+ Store rainwater in barrels outside for garden usage rather than relying on a hose.

+ A garden sprinkler uses an incredible amount of water (the same amount in half an hour that four people use in a day!). Use it sparingly or, better still, use a watering can instead.

REDUCING HEATING BILLS

There are many forms of insulation you can install that will make your heating system more efficient.

Checklist

✦ Keep your thermostat no higher than 64.5–68 degrees F. Turning it down by 2 degrees won't make much difference to your comfort.

✦ Install attic insulation, or if you already have attic insulation top it up to the level of the joists if necessary. The recommended thickness for attic insulation is 6–10 inches. This form of insulation can save you as much as 20–25 percent on your heating bills (*see* pages 125–28).

✦ Cavity insulation is expensive but worth doing as it will pay for itself within around five years.

✦ Drafts can lose up to 15 per cent of the heat in your home. Fit draft blockers to doors (*see* pages 129–32) and windows (*see* pages 132–33). You can also use mastic between baseboards and floors in order to stop drafts at floor level.

✦ Fit reflective panels behind radiators on outside walls to reduce heat loss (*see* page 124).

✦ If you have double glazing, radiators can be fitted anywhere. Consider moving them so they are back to back on internal walls, to lessen the piping needed.

FITTING THERMOSTATIC VALVES

Although most modern heating systems have a central thermostat that switches the power off when the house has reached the required temperature, you can go one better and fit individual valves to radiators for more control in each room. The kitchen, for example, is usually quite hot anyway so the valve here can be set lower.

Fitting radiator valves

Shut off the system and drain down the boiler. Leave the water to cool for a while and then switch off the shut-off valve. Place one end of a garden hose over the drain plug and the other end into a bucket. Open the drain plug to release all the water (*see* page 15). Any trapped water can be removed by opening the bleed valves on the radiators, starting with the one furthest away from the drain plug.

Put old cloths and a container under the pipe and around the old valve that is being replaced, then use an adjustable wrench to remove the radiator union nut. Next use the wrench to remove the cap nut and olive from the bottom of the valve, then lift it off (1). (You may have to cut the olive off with pipe cutters.) The thermostatic valve may be a different length than the old one so make any necessary alterations to the pipework.

Then slide on the cap nut and new olive (2). If the new valve has a different tail than the old one fit the new tail using a radiator valve wrench.

Wrap plumber's tape around the thread before fitting the valve. Half-tighten it to the union first, then the cap nut (3). Finally fit the cap and finish tightening the union valve then the cap nut (4).

1. Remove the radiator union nut then lift off the whole valve.

2. After altering the pipework, slide on the cap nut and new olive.

3. Fit the valve and then half-tighten it to the union nut.

4. Fit the thermostatic control cap before tightening everything.

INSULATING PIPES

All pipes—hot and cold—that are exposed to cold air should be insulated.

The basic technique

Split-foam tubing is the most common type of pipe insulation. The split enables the tube to be fitted over the pipe easily. Cut tubes to length using a craft knife then slide them over the pipework (1). Any joints can be sealed using insulating tape (2). To turn a corner, you will need to make a miter cut. Mark the 45-degree angle on the tube using a square and cut the tube. Do the same with the next piece to complete the angle (3) then seal them together with tape.

1. Simply slide the tubes onto the pipework.

2. Use insulating tape to seal joints.

3. Cut 45-degree angles in the tubing to turn a corner.

Insulating a T-junction

You will need to cut corresponding V-shaped notches into the three pieces of tubing that will cover the T-junction. Then simply fit them and cover the joints with insulating tape.

Cut V-shapes to fit the tubing over a T-junction.

Insulating curved piping

To insulate a piece of curved piping, you will need to cut a series of small V-shaped notches into one side of the tube. This will ensure that it doesn't wrinkle when it is bent round the pipe. You can then use tape to seal the joints.

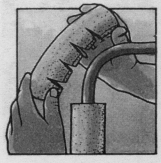

Cut V-shaped notches into the tubing to fit it around a curve.

REFLECTING HEAT FROM A RADIATOR

Fitting reflective panels behind a radiator will reduce heat loss a lot, as around 25 per cent of radiators' heat is lost to the wall behind.

Fitting a reflective panel

Turn off the radiator and measure it, noting where the brackets are. Use a sharp craft knife to cut the lining to size, slightly smaller than the radiator. Cut slots into the lining so it can fit over the brackets (1). Cover the back of the panel with fungicidal wallpaper paste then position it (2). Smooth it to the wall using a radiator roller. Let the paste dry then turn the radiator back on.

1. Cut slots in the lining so it can slide over the radiator's brackets.

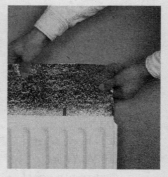

2. Slide the panel into its position behind the radiator.

INSULATING AN ATTIC

The two main types of insulation for use in roofs are blanket insulation, which comes in rolls, and loose fill insulation, which can be bought in bags. The recommended depth for roof insulation is 6–10 inches but don't worry about adding extra, especially as 25–30 per cent of heat loss in a house occurs through an uninsulated roof.

Before you start to lay either type of insulation you should prepare the area properly by sealing any large gaps around piping, vents or wiring with flexible mastic. Also make sure that you have a proper working platform (such as scaffolding boards that can be laid directly across the joists) and adequate lighting (hang a temporary light up if necessary).

Laying blanket insulation

This type of insulation is compressed when packed, so it will expand when rolled out. This means you should remove the packaging only once it is in the attic and you are ready to use it. Trim the ends of each length to a chamfer shape in order to allow airflow from the eaves then roll them out (1—page 126).

TIP: Make sure to wear gloves, protective clothing and goggles when working with roof insulating material.

Lift any electrical cabling so that you can roll the insulation underneath it. You should also ensure that any light cases or lamp fittings that protrude into the attic are not covered, by simply trimming the insulation closely around them using a craft knife or pair of scissors (2).

1. Roll out the lengths.

To ensure that no heat escapes, it is best to lay a second layer of the insulation at right angles to the first, over the top of the joists (3). Make sure you also cut a piece of the insulation to fit over the attic door. You can attach this using adhesive. Foam draft blockers can also be fitted to the edges of the door for extra draftproofing.

2. Cut around any light cases as well as lamp fittings.

3. Lay a second layer of insulation.

Laying loose fill insulation

When laying loose insulation you must fix strips of plywood or thick cardboard between the joists in order to avoid the eaves getting clogged up with bits of the insulation. Where there are pipes, create a bridge with a piece of cardboard so that air can easily circulate around them (1).

You will need at least a 6-inch depth of fill to create the insulation, so if your joists are very shallow you should attach battening to them so that they will still be able to support any necessary boarding for walking on. Then simply pour in the insulation, spread it and tamp it down level using a timber offcut (2).

1. Create a cardboard bridge around any piping in the attic.

2. Tamp down the insulation using a piece of wood.

Insulating a sloping roof

If you are going to use the attic as a proper room you will also need to insulate the sloping part of the roof. First make sure the roof and its tiles are sound. As condensation often occurs between rafters that have been insulated it is important to provide a 2-inch gap between the insulation and tiles for ventilation purposes. The ridge and eaves should also be ventilated. Blanket or sheet insulation can be used between the rafters but you should also include a vapor barrier on the warm side of the insulation, either by using foil-backed blanket insulation or by covering unbacked insulation with polythene sheets stapled to the rafters. Once you've fitted the insulation you can cover the rafters with plasterboard to create the final layer that can then be decorated.

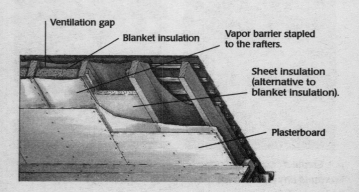

Ventilation gap

Blanket insulation

Vapor barrier stapled to the rafters.

Sheet insulation (alternative to blanket insulation).

Plasterboard

DRAFTPROOFING DOORS AND WINDOWS

Adding draftproofing to external doors and windows can help cut down on the amount of drafts reaching the inside of your home.

Fitting a door draft blocker

If the gap between the bottom of the door and the floor is quite large you should consider fitting a draft blocker. There are many different types (*see* below), but they are each easily screwed to the bottom of the door. To do this you need to place the rigid plastic or metal part of the blocker along the bottom of the door and lower it until the sealer strip covers the gap below the door. Mark two screw holes with an awl then screw the blocker into position.

+ **Brush seal blocker** This is made up of a long nylon brush set into a metal or plastic extrusion. It is the only type that can be used on sliding doors as well as hinged ones (*see* page 130).

+ **Automatic blocker** This has a plastic strip and extruded clip that are both spring-loaded so they lift off the floor when the door is opened. When the door closes, the blocker is pressed down to the floor by a stop screwed to the doorframe (*see* page 130).

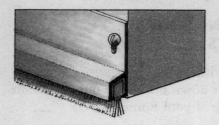

Brush seal blocker

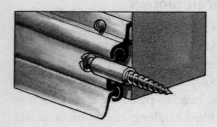

Automatic blocker

Flexible arch

Door kit

✦ **Flexible arch** This has an arched vinyl insert that presses against the bottom edge of the door. For an external door you will need one that has additional underseals to prevent rain from seeping underneath it. As this is one of the deepest blockers, you may have to plane the bottom of the door in order to fit it.

✦ **Door kit** This is the best solution for an external door, as it is specifically designed to shed rainwater as well as keep drafts out. It has an aluminum rain deflector that screws to the face of the door, as well as a weather bar with a rubber or plastic draft blocker.

Sealing a keyhole and mail slot

Once an external door has a draft blocker fitted, you don't want unnecessary drafts escaping into the house through the keyhole and mail slot.

You can fix a coverplate over the external keyhole. This is simply screwed into place (1—page 132).

There are also hinged flaps or brush frames that can be fitted over the inside of a mail slot (some blockers have both). Simply mark where the screw holes should be positioned and then screw the draft blocker securely to the door (2—page 132).

1. Screw the coverplate over the keyhole.

2. Screw the draft blocker to the door.

Fitting a window draft blocker

As most casement windows are made of wood they will warp over time and become ill-fitting, causing drafts that whistle through the house. A plastic, self-adhesive molded draft blocker can be fitted to eliminate these drafts.

SEALING SASH WINDOWS

Sash windows are harder to seal because the top and bottom need to be free to move up and down. Some restoration companies will fit a system of nylon brushes around the frame for you. To tackle sealing a sash window yourself, use a brush seal on the sides and a vinyl tubular strip on the horizontal gaps. Cut the strip with a junior hacksaw to fit the frame part. Some products have a self-adhesive backing while others will need to be held in place with small panel pins. Make sure that the strip is positioned so that the edge fits snugly against the adjacent frame part.

This type of draft blocker normally comes in a double roll, so you will need to split it into two single strips before you fit it (1). Then clean the surfaces that you will be putting the blocker onto before peeling off the backing paper from the strip (2).

1. Split the blocker into two single strips.

Working from the top right-hand corner, gently press the blocker strip into place on the outside of the fixed window frames. You will need to leave a 1-inch trimming edge on each piece. Cut the ends of the lengths to form 45-degree angles in order to create neat joints in the corners (3). Then shut the window and secure it firmly to allow the strips to stick properly.

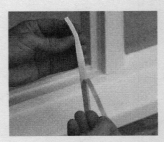

2. Peel the backing paper off the strip.

3. Cut 45-degree angles to create neat corners.